ANECDOTES

Concerning the Famous

JOHN REINHOLD PATKUL:

OR, AN

AUTHENTIC RELATION

Of what passed

Betwixt HIM and his CONFESSOR,

The Night before and at his Execution.

Translated from the Original MANUSCRIPT, never yet printed.

LONDON:
Printed for A. MILLAR, 1761.

In the interest of creating a more extensive selection of rare historical book reprints, we have chosen to reproduce this title even though it may possibly have occasional imperfections such as missing and blurred pages, missing text, poor pictures, markings, dark backgrounds and other reproduction issues beyond our control. Because this work is culturally important, we have made it available as a part of our commitment to protecting, preserving and promoting the world's literature. Thank you for your understanding.

INTRODUCTION.

NO kind of writing can be more interesting to a reader of taste and humanity, than authentic relations of what has happened to men, eminent for their abilities, and unfortunate by their virtue. We, therefore, flatter ourselves, that the public will receive with pleasure the following account of the famous Patkul, renowned all over Europe for defending the rights of his native country, and still more memorable by his tragical death.

The original copy of this account has never yet been printed: and this is the first time a translation of it into English has been attempted. It was drawn up by the Lutheran minister, chaplain of a regiment, who attended that unhappy man in his last moments, the night before

before his death, and at the place of execution.

Many of the particulars, disclosed by the penitent to his confessor, will be found entirely new: they are at the same time equally curious and important. None of the historians, not even the celebrated biographer of Charles the Twelfth, seems to have been acquainted with them; so that they will serve in some places to rectify his mistakes, as in others they will confirm the truth of what he has advanced.

To render this narrative as complete as possible, we have here brought together, under one view, the several particulars concerning Patkul, that lie scattered in different parts of monsieur de Voltaire's work.

John Reinhold Patkul was, by birth, a Livonian, and descended from a considerable family in that country;

country; which is the finest and most fertile province of the North. It belonged of old to the knights of the Teutonic order. The Russians, the Poles, the Swedes, had alternately disputed the possession of it; but Sweden had carried it from the rest near an hundred years ago; and it had been, at last, solemnly ceded to her by the treaty of Oliva.

Charles the Eleventh, who had treated his other subjects with great severity, was not more indulgent to the Livonians: he had stripped them of their privileges, and of a part of their estates.

Patkul was deputed by the nobility of his province to carry their complaints to the throne. The harangue he pronounced before his master was at once respectful and bold, full of that manly eloquence, which calamity, supported by courage,

rage, never fails to infpire: but fovereigns, for the moft part, look on thofe public harangues as only vain ceremonies, which it is cuftomary to fuffer, without paying any regard to them. However Charles, who could diffemble when he did not give up the reins to his anger, laid his hand gently on Patkul's fhoulder, "You have fpoke for your country as a brave man fhould," faid the king to him: "I efteem you for it. Proceed." But a few days after, he had him declared guilty of high-treafon, and, as fuch, condemned to die. Patkul, who had concealed himfelf, fled. He carried with him into Poland his refentment of this ufage; and was admitted afterwards into the prefence of king Auguftus. Charles the Eleventh was then dead; but the fentence againft Patkul, and his indignation at it, ftill fubfifted. He reprefented to the Polifh monarch, how eafily the conqueft of Livonia might be effected; the people desperate, ready to shake off the Swedish yoke; her king a child, and incapable of defending himself. These sollicitations were well received by a prince whom this conquest had already tempted.

After the celebrated battle of Narva, in which Charles the Twelfth, with only eight thousand Swedes, defeated fourscore thousand Moscovites, the king of Poland had reason to fear, that his enemy, who had now conquered them and the Danes, would quickly fall upon him. He therefore entered into a stricter union than ever with the Czar: and these two princes agreed upon an interview to concert their future measures.

After having passed the winter in the neighbourhood of Narva, Charles appeared in Livonia, near that very city of Riga, which king Auguſtus had beſieged in vain. The Saxon troops were poſted along the river Duna, which is very broad in that place; and Charles, who was on the other ſide, had that paſſage to diſpute with them. The Saxons were not headed by their prince, then indiſpoſed; but by marſhal Stenaw, who commanded in chief. Under him were prince Ferdinand, duke of Courland, and the ſame Patkul, who now defended his country, with his ſword, againſt Charles the Twelfth, after having maintained its privileges by his pen, at the hazard of his life, againſt Charles the Eleventh.

Every one knows, that the Saxons loſt this battle, and that Charles went on with interrupted ſucceſs; till, in the end, he compelled Auguſtus to abdicate the throne of Poland, and his ſubjects to chuſe another

ther king in his stead. A little before that memorable event, Patkul had entered into the service of Russia, and been distinguished by the Czar with the title of his ambassador in Saxony. The commission intrusted to him there, was to prevail with Augustus to meet the Czar at Grodno, that they might confer once more on the state of their affairs. This conference was but just ended, and the Czar gone to extinguish a rebellion which threatened him at Astracan, when king Augustus ordered Patkul to be seized at Dresden. All Europe stood surprised, that, contrary to the law of nations, and, in appearance, contrary to his own interests, he had dared to imprison the ambassador of the only prince who protected him.

The secret spring of so strange an event, as our author learnt from the late marshal Saxe, son of king Augustus,

gustus, was this. Patkul, proscribed in Sweden for having defended the privileges of Livonia, his native country, had been a general under Augustus; but his proud and active spirit, ill agreeing with the haughtiness of general Flemming, the king's favorite, more imperious and fiery than himself, he had gone over to the service of the Czar, whose general and ambassador to Augustus he then was. Of a very penetrating spirit, he soon discovered that the views of Flemming, and of the chancellor of Saxony, were to propose a peace to the Swedish monarch on any terms whatever: upon this he immediately formed the design of being before-hand with them, by bringing about a reconciliation betwixt the Czar and Sweden. The chancellor, however, having traced out his project, obtained leave to seize and secure his person. King Augustus assured the Czar that Patkul was a traitor,

traitor, who betrayed them both; and yet his only crime was having served his new master too well: but an unseasonable service is often rewarded as if it were a piece of treachery.

At last king Augustus, now a fugitive in Poland, deprived at once of his kingdom and of his electorate, wrote a letter with his own hand, to beg a peace of Charles. The fourth article, of the very hard terms on which he granted that peace, is the only one with which we are here concerned.

Augustus shall deliver up to me all the deserters who have entered into his service; particularly, and by name, John Patkul.

The sacrificing of Patkul must have occasioned a severe struggle in his breast. On one side, the Czar

loudly

loudly reclaimed this man as his ambaffador : on the other, Charles demanded with threats, that he fhould be put into his hands. Patkul was then confined in the caftle of Koenigftein in Saxony. Auguftus imagined he might fatisfy Charles the Twelfth, and his own honor at the fame time. He fent fome guards to deliver up this unhappy man to the Swedifh troops; but he had tranfmitted before-hand a fecret order to the governor of Koenigftein, to let his prifoner efcape. Patkul's ill fortune prevailed over the care that was taken to fave him. The governor, knowing him to be very rich, would oblige him to purchafe his liberty; but the prifoner ftill depending on the law of nations, and acquainted with the intentions of Auguftus in his favor, refufed to buy what he hoped to obtain for nothing. During this interval arrived the guards that were ordered to feize him :

him: they delivered him immediately to four Swedish captains, who carried him at first to the head-quarters at Altranstad, where he continued three months, bound to a stake with a heavy chain of iron. From thence he was transported to Casimir. There, Charles the Twelfth, forgetting his quality of ambassador from the Czar, ordered him to be tried with the utmost rigor by a court-martial.

About this very time he was to have married a Saxon lady; a woman of quality, of virtue, and beauty. The reader will hear more of her from his own mouth, in the following relation, which cannot fail of exciting at once pity and horror in the highest degree: pity, for the sufferings of a man, whose greatest crime was his having appeared in the defence of his country; and horror,

horror, at the unrelenting cruelty of a monarch, who, in punishing it, consulted only his own arbitrary temper, and the hatred he bore his enemies.

AN

AN

AUTHENTIC ACCOUNT

Of the BEHAVIOUR of

JOHN REINHOLD PATKUL,

The Night before his Death, and at the Place of Execution.

PATKUL had been a prisoner for some months, under the guard of Meyerfeldt's regiment, uncertain of his fate, and in continual apprehensions from the inflexible temper of the king of Sweden. At last, on the 28th of September, in the year 1707, towards evening, accompanied by thirty soldiers, he was delivered into the custody of the regiment of dragoons, commanded by colonel Nicholas Hielm. On the very next, which was St. Michael's-day, my colonel took me aside, and communicating to me the dreadful secret that Patkul was to die the day fol-

following, ordered me to inform him of his approaching fate, and prepare him to meet death as a good christian should. Immediately after evening-service I went to his prison, where I found him lying on his bed. The first compliments over, I entered upon the melancholy duty of my profession, by asking pardon for my intrusion, and by saying, that a heart afflicted as his was, must doubtless have need of consolation from the word of God. He answered, that he was delighted and obliged by this mark of my attention, and that no visits were so agreeable to him as those from persons in holy orders; adding, Are there any news abroad ? To which I replied, That I had something of importance to acquaint him with, provided we were left alone. He immediately raised himself up on the bed : and I, turning to the officer who had him in charge, told him the colonel's orders were, that I should be alone with his prisoner.

The

The officer having withdrawn, Patkul grasping both my hands in his, cried out, in a voice to soften the hardest heart,—"Ah! my dear Pastor, what are you to declare? what I have to hear?"

"I bring you," replied I, "the same tidings that the prophet brought to king Hezekiah: *Set thine house in order, for thou must die.* To-morrow, by this time, thou shalt be no longer in the number of the living!" At this terrible warning, he bowed himself upon his bed, and melted into a flood of tears.

I then attempted to comfort him the best I could, by saying, that as he was a man well instructed in several sciences, and particularly conversant in the sacred scriptures, he must, without all doubt, have often meditated on this subject; and that I therefore hoped it would not have plunged him into so much sorrow. "Yes," cried he, "I know, alas! too well,

well, that we muſt all die; but,— (and then the tears ſtreamed again from his eyes) the death prepared for me will be too cruel, and inſupportable."

In order to calm his mind by degrees, I aſſured him, that the manner of his death was to me totally unknown; but, believing that he would prepare himſelf for it, as every good man ought, I was ſure that his ſoul would be received into the number of happy ſpirits. Here he roſe up, and, folding his hands together, " Merciful Jeſus!" he cried, " let me then die the death of the juſt." A little after, with his face inclined towards the wall, where ſtood his bed, he broke into this ſoliloquy: " Auguſtus! O Auguſtus, what muſt be thy lot one day? Muſt not thou be reſponſible then for all the crimes by thee committed? Alas! the revolution in Sweden and Livonia is the ſource of my misfortunes."

I intreated him to lay aside all wordly confiderations, as particularly difagreeable in themfelves, and moft unfuitable to the profpect before him; that he might devote his thoughts entirely to another, and never-ending life; and thus employ his few remaining moments for the peace and repofe of his foul. His anfwer was, "Alas! dear fir, my heart, this wretched heart, which is all over one inveterate ulcer, full of unfound humours, cannot know reft or quiet, till their malignity is difcharged: fuffer me, therefore, to tell you what it is big with, and what fo much torments it.

"That *reduction*, which hath impoverifhed fo many families, is the fole caufe of the crime whereof I am accufed. The late * king faid to me, one day, in terms of much kindnefs, Patkul, maintain the rights of your country like a man of honor, and with all the fpirit you are

* Charles XI.

capable

capable of. My God, what part was I to act after such a declaration?—but my enemies turned it all to my disadvantage. May heaven pardon Hieftner! He contributed much to my destruction; for in the beginning he seduced, in the middle of our affairs he imposed upon me, and in the end became my persecutor. Bergenhielm too did me all the mischief in his power; but he was obliged to follow his orders. O Sweden! Sweden! I quitted thee, neither dancing nor singing; thou knowest it, O my God! What else was left me to do?—To hide myself under-ground was impossible; to bury myself in a convent, against the religion I profess; and amongst the allies of the king, there was no retreat to be hoped for.

" It has been said that I joined myself to his enemies: that I was therefore the cause of this fatal war. But, what a consequence! I spent my melancholy hours

a wretched

a wretched exile, not a counsellor, or adviser; a part, of which I was never thought capable, as in truth I was not.

"Before my arrival in Saxony every thing was already planned; the alliance with Muscovy signed; the measures with Denmark agreed upon; and I, at that time, in no degree of estimation ———."

At this pause in his discourse I gently reprimanded him; because what he had been saying was no longer seasonable, and yet he gave himself up entirely to the consideration of mere wordly matters.— But seizing my hand, he begged I would grant him a few moments more to disburthen his heart; and then, cried he, I will not lose an instant longer. "Of what country are you, dear Sir?" "A Swede," I replied, "and born at Stockholm." "I am rejoiced to hear it," said he: "I wish to have some part in the remembrance of your countrymen, and that they may know

the

the truth of my deplorable fate. My inclinations were always to ferve Sweden, however the contrary opinion has prevailed.—Yet more;

"I can affirm, without vanity, wretched as I am at this moment, that the *Churfurſt* of Brandenburg, owed his title of king of Pruſſia to the ſervices I did him. He himſelf will acknowledge it; as he formerly, in recompenſe of thoſe good offices, would have given me a conderable ſum of money. I thanked him, and rejected the offer; adding, that the moſt valuable reward I wiſhed for, was to regain the king of Sweden's favor by his interceſſion. This he promiſed, and tried every method poſſible to ſucceed, by his miniſter at Stockholm, count Dona: but in that court the gate of mercy was ſhut againſt me.

" After this I laboured ſo much for the intereſt of the late emperor in his Spaniſh affairs,

* Prince-elector.

affairs, that I brought about what any other man could scarcely have effected; may I be allowed to say so without ostentation. The emperor, on his part, as an acknowledgment of this service, gave me an assignment for fifty thousand crowns, which I humbly laid at his feet; and making him a low bow, begged a reward of another kind. He asked what else he could do for me? I replied, that all this money would profit me nothing, while I remained in disgrace at the court of Sweden; and therefore I implored his Imperial majesty's recommendation of me to the king's favor. This request he immediately granted, and gave his orders accordingly, but in vain. All my hopes there vanished into smoke. Yet, not to lose any opportunity possible, I went to Moscow while the Swedish ambassadors were at that court.—You have doubtless heard of the thing," said he. "It is true," I replied; "and as I had then the honor of being preacher to the legation, I was often

ten an eye-witness of the court you paid to the ambassadors."

"How!" cried he, "were you there at that juncture?—yes, methinks I recollect your face:" and then he went on to inform me, that his whole application was employed to obtain that favor which had been so frequently refused him: but the mediation of the Czar had no effect. "On the contrary," said this unfortunate man, "having secretly learnt, that an order from the king was sent to his ambassadors to find me out, and insist upon my being delivered into their hands, I was obliged to fly, and hide myself from the world. During these negociations it was confidently given out, that I had dealt privately with the Czar to break the peace: nothing could be more unjust. Carlovitz, a creature of king Augustus, and others, to whose names I am no stranger, were those that instigated him to take such a resolution. For my part, I was ever inclined

clined to peace, and employed, for that end, every means in my power; propoſing, as a ſatisfaction to the king, that he ſhould have Courland, Poliſh Livonia, and a great part of Samogitia, if theſe conceſſions might have induced him to make peace. It was at firſt believed, that the Czar would never ſubmit to ſuch conditions; but, on my frequent and preſſing remonſtrances, he gave his conſent, and even thanked me for my good offices. The king of Sweden, however, would hearken to no terms; and this only can hinder the Swediſh priſoners at Moſcow from confeſſing, that I diſtributed among them at leaſt an hundred thouſand crowns, to ſhew the ardent deſire I had, by all ways, to regain their ſovereign's favor and grace.—Ah! would to heaven I had been equally in earneſt to obtain the grace of God!" At theſe words another ſhower of tears fell from his eyes, and he remained for ſome moments ſilent, and overwhelmed with grief.

I used my most affectionate endeavors to comfort him, with the assurance that this grace would not be denied him, provided he spent the few hours still left in earnestly imploring it; for the door of Heaven's mercy was never shut, tho' that of men might be cruelly so.

" This," replied he, " this is my true consolation ;—for thou art God, not man to be angry for ever. But alas! it is now my confusion, to have fought with more sollicitude the means of rendering service to men than of serving God.

" Above all, I curse the hour of my knowing Augustus, and of my connections with him. May God turn his heart from its insidious purposes. Void of all faith and honor, he betrays the very ministers he employs.

" Reflect only on what he did after the peace with Sweden was concluded. At that very time he writ me a letter, dated

the

the sixteenth of December, in which he ordered me to inform the Czar, that the Swedes were dispersed in different places, waiting in full security, till their arms, all hacked and broken, could be repaired; and that their officers were sent away, some to raise new levies, and others about other necessary services. This, therefore, said he, was the favorable moment for the Czar to make an irruption into Saxony with all his force, that he might fall upon and destroy them at once. On his part, he would underhand prevent the workmen, employed in mending the arms, from doing what was expected of them.

"To this I sent him in answer, that I would no longer concern myself with his affairs, and that it was full time to give over all such perfidious contrivances. But tho he was displeased with my reply, he still discovered to me, from time to time, his wicked purposes, and tried to engage me in them, which I always plainly refused to do.

"In a letter to me, a most extraordinary piece of treachery was planned out; and the letter concluded with these words: *Augustus has gained more by one single bunting, than Charles by so many splendid victories.* I stand astonished when I reflect on such inhuman machinations, and render thanks to God, who *saved the king from several ambushes that have been laid for him.*"

"Good heaven!" cried I, "who would ever more trust to Augustus?" "Ah!" replied the prisoner, "a notorious atheist like him, who has no fear of God on his mind, can such a man shew any regard to his plighted faith?

"The late emperor, in a letter to me, desired that I would endeavor, by gentle insinuation, to divert him from his extravagant courses. I was bold enough to shew him that letter: he read it, and with a contemptuous smile said to me, "Let the old man trouble his head about purgatory: he is in the right, he will be there before me." His mother too employed me on the same errand. I again undertook the part;—and what has been my reward? I am at last plunged into an abyss of misery.

"While he was at Warschou, and heard the king was advancing to attack him, he found himself extremely distressed. He was absolutely without money, and therefore obliged to dismiss some of his troops. He had recourse to my assistance, and intreated me, for the love of God, to borrow whatever sum I could. I undertook the thing, and procured him four hundred thousand crowns. What use did he make of this supply? The very day afterwards he lavished away fifty thousand crowns on trinkets and jewels, which he gave in presents to some of his women.

"I was infinitely concerned that he should have squandered the money in this strange manner, as my orders from the Czar, my principal, were not to trust him

with

with a farthing. I told him plainly my thoughts of the matter; and by my importunity prevailed, that the Jews should take back their toys, and return the money they had been paid for them. The ladies were enraged; and he swore to himself that I should, one time or other, suffer for what I had done: there indeed, he kept his word. Would to God he had always done so with those he employed! but that just God will repay him one day all his misdeeds.

"I am afraid, dear Sir, that this talk, and all these particulars, are irksome to you, and you may be wanted elsewhere on other business." I answered, that I would be with him again in a moment. "Be so," said he; "and above all intreat the colonel, if you please, that he would give his orders for our being alone together, that I may not be disturbed in these last moments, which should be sacred to devotion: and this I shall esteem a very particular favor." I promised to obtain what he desired, and then withdrew.

At seven in the evening I returned; and the officer being retired, his prisoner accosted me, with a smiling air, and an appearance of much tranquillity: "Welcome, dear Sir, and now I look upon you as my better angel. The weight that lay heavy and oppressive on my heart is removed, and I already feel a sensible change wrought in my mind. I am ready to die: death is more eligible than the solitude of a long imprisonment. Would to heaven only, that the kind of it were less cruel. Can you, my dear confessor, inform me in what way I am to suffer?" My answer, as before, was, that it had not been communicated to me; but that the whole would pass over without noise, for that hitherto only the colonel and myself had notice of it.

"That," replied he, "I esteem as a favor, but have you seen the sentence? Or must I die, without being either heard or condemned? My apprehensions are, of being put to intolerable tortures." I comforted

forted him in the kindeſt manner I could; but he was his own beſt comforter from the word of God, with which he was familiarly acquainted; quoting, among other paſſages, theſe words in Greek: *We muſt enter into the kingdom of heaven thro many tribulations.*

He then called for pen and ink; which being brought, he intreated me to write down what he ſhould dictate. I did ſo, as follows:

"Teſtamentum, or, my laſt will, as to the diſpoſition of my effects after my death.

"I. His majeſty king Auguſtus, having firſt examined his conſcience thoroughly, will be ſo juſt as to pay back to my relations the ſum he owes me; which, being liquidated, will amount to fifty thouſand crowns: and as my relations are here in the ſervice of Sweden, that monarch will probably obtain it for them." At this he
ſaid,

said, "Let us stop here a little; I will quickly return to finish this will: but now let us address ourselves to God by prayer." Prayers being ended, "And now," cried he, "I find myself yet better, yet in a quieter frame of mind. Oh! were my death less dreadful, with what pleasure would I expiate all my guilt by embracing it! Is the king of a merciful disposition?" "Yes," replied I, "and we are thankful to heaven for giving us a pious and gracious sovereign." "That," said my penitent, "is the capital virtue, and it has all the others attending upon it. His ministers too, are they remarkable for humanity? Is count Piper a man of piety?" I answered to these different questions in the affirmative; adding, that he had given proofs of it that were no wise equivocal. "Thanks be to God then," cried he," I shall not be exposed to feel beyond what justice requires. Happy is that kingdom where equity and piety reign."

He next entered upon a conversation concerning the affairs of Sweden, the universities, the men of learning, and particularly the professor at Hall, named Franchen, and a certain doctor, Breithaupt; asking me, at the same time, my opinion of the religion professed by the Pietists; and where I myself had been educated—ending the whole with a profound sigh!

"Yes!" cried he — "I have friends in different places, who will weep over my deplorable fate. What will the mother of the king of Prussia say? What will be the grief of the countess Levolde, who attends upon her? but particularly, and above all, what thoughts must arise in the bosom of HER, to whom my faith is plighted? Unhappy woman! the news of my death will be fatal to her peace of mind. My dear Pastor, may I venture to beg one favor of you?" I assured him he might command every service, every office of humanity in my power. "Have the goodness then," continued he, pres-

fing

fing my hand—the moment I am no more—to write—alas! how will you set about it? a letter to madam Einfeidelern—the lady I am promifed to—Let her know I die her's—inform her fully, of my unhappy fate! Send her my laft and eternal farewel! My death is in truth difgraceful; but my manner of meeting it will, I hope, by heaven's and your affiftance, render it holy and bleffed. This news will be her only confolation. Add farther, dear Sir, that I thanked her with my lateft breath, for the fincere affection fhe bore me. May fhe live long and happy: this is my dying wifh."

I gave him my hand in promife that I would faithfully perform all he defired. At this he drew out his purfe, wrapping the money he took from thence in two or three different pieces of paper: "Tomorrow," faid he, "I fhall think no more of the things of this world:" and would have had me accept of one of thofe papers, in which were an hundred ducats.

I mo-

I modestly excused myself from receiving them, as the little services I had done him could merit no such present. "Ah!" cried he, "how often, for a trivial worldly matter, have I given a thousand? and the service you are doing me cannot be repaid with all the gold on earth. However, to shew my further gratitude, I present you with a treasure that I have kept sacred above all things else——my New Testament in Greek, with the version of Montanus. It has been my companion in all my misery; and is now in the hands of major Grothusen, from whom you will receive it." I made him my acknowledgments, and promised never to part with such a present during my life.

Afterwards he took up another book: "This," said he, "is of my own writing. Keep it in remembrance of me, and as a proof of my true regard for religion. I could wish it might have the good fortune to be presented to the king, that he may
be

be convinced, with what little foundation I have been accused of atheism." Taking it from his hand I assured him, that my colonel would not fail to present it, as soon as an opportunity offered. "Ah!" said he, "it would be some poor satisfaction, if my book might be more fortunate than its author: and I cannot forbear applying to it, what Ovid said of old to his *De Tristibus*, when he was sending the volume to Augustus, from the place of his banishment: Go, little book, and procure for me what I myself could not obtain."

The rest of his time was employed in prayer, which he went thro with a very fervent devotion: and mentioning the vanity of this world, "God is my witness," said he, "that, in the midst of those pleasures it spreads out for us, my heart was ever penetrated with remorse; and now the weight that pressed me down to earth is entirely removed from it. World, farewel! sick of all sublunary vanities, I have often and earnestly meditated a retreat;

but

but without effect, having been too far engaged in the stream to be able to turn back. I return thee thanks, O Jesus! that my chains are broken, that my soul is set free by the hand of Charles the Twelfth. My God! the truth of what St. Paul says is manifested in me, *That all worketh for good to those who are loved of God.*

"But as it grows late I am afraid, dear Sir, that I detain you too long. Let not the time appear tedious, I conjure you." I assured him of the satisfaction I took in doing my duty, and began again to pray for him with new fervor. Our devotions being ended, he asked me whether he should not try to take some repose; adding, that for a long time he had not been refreshed with a moment's sleep, and that he felt his spirits quite exhausted, as he had neither ate nor drank any thing the whole day. "By this my wearied faculties may be recruited; and to-morrow I shall stand in need of all my strength!"

strength!" To which I assented; and having agreed upon the hour I should return, I left him alone for the rest of this his last night.

On the thirtieth of September I was again with him at four in the morning. The moment he heard my salutation he arose, and rendering thanks to God, assured me he had not slept so soundly for a long time. We went to prayers; and in truth his piety, and devout frame of mind, were worthy of admiration.

About the hour of six he said he would begin his confession, before the din and clamors of the people without could rise to disturb his thoughts. He then kneeled down, and went thro his confession in a manner truly edifying. The beginning of it especially was remarkable, when he made use of these words of Judah: *What shall I say, O Lord? or how shall I utter myself? God hath found out the iniquities of his servant.* After having received the holy

holy communion, he sung a psalm or two, but dwelt with singular pleasure on this verse: *May thy spirit comfort me; may thy wounds be my healing.*

The sun beginning to appear above the horizon, he looked out at the window, saying, "*Salve festa dies!* This is my wedding-day. I looked, alas! for another, but this is the happier; for to-day shall my soul be introduced by her heavenly bridegroom into the assembly of the blessed!"

He then turned to me, and begged to be informed whether I yet knew in what way he was to die? I answered, as before: and he conjured me, by the sacred name of Jesus, not to forsake him; for that he should find in my company some consolation even in the midst of tortures.

He looked again through the window, crying out, "My dear pastor, they are already putting to the horses. They are

in

in haste; and, heaven be praised, to me likewise the time appears too long. I have not now a wish to live." Casting his eye on the paper that lay upon the table, "This will," said he, "can never be finished." When I asked him, whether he would put his name to what was already written? "No," replied he, "with a deep sigh, I will write that hated name no more. My relations will find their account in another place: salute them from me." He then addressed himself again to God in prayer, till

The lieutenant entered to conduct him to the coach. He wrapped himself up in his cloak, and requested me, as he went along, not to abandon him. When I assured him that I would not, he advanced towards the coach, and made me go into it before him. We went forward a great pace, guarded by an hundred horsemen. On the way he embraced and kissed me, requesting me again not to forget the promise I had made him.

Being arrived at the place of execution, we found it surrounded by three hundred foot-soldiers; but at the sight of the *stakes* and *wheels*, his horror is not to be described. Clasping me in his arms, "Beg of God," he exclaimed, "that my soul may not be thrown into despair amidst these tortures! I comforted, I adjured him to fix his thoughts on the death of Jesus Christ, who, for our sins, was nailed to a cross.

At this he was taken out of the coach; and while they were knocking off his fetters, *Lamb of God,* cried he, *who takest away the sins of the world, have mercy upon me!*

Being now on the spot where he was to suffer, the captain proclaimed aloud:

"Be it known to all, it is by command of his majesty, our sovereign, that this man, who has been a traitor to his country, shall be broken on the wheel alive,

and

and then his body shall be divided into four quarters, that he may serve for an example to all such criminals." At the word traitor, he shrugged up his shoulders, casting his eyes mournfully towards heaven, and then said, " Whither must I go ?" The executioner pointing to the fatal spot, he bid the man do his duty well, and put into his hands some money, which he had got ready for that purpose.

He then stretched himself out upon the ground ; and while they were stripping him naked, he begged me to pray that God would have mercy on him, and bear up his soul in this agony. I did so : and turning to all the spectators, said to them, " Brethren, join with me in prayer for this unhappy man." " Yes," cried he, " assist me all of you with your supplications to heaven."

Here the executioner gave him the first stroke. His cries were terrible. " O Jesus ! Jesus, have mercy upon me !" This

cruel

cruel scene was much lengthened out, and of the utmost horror; for as the headsman had no skill in his business, the wretch under his hands received upwards of fifteen several blows, with each of which were intermixed the most piteous groans, and invocations of the name of God. At length, after two strokes given on the breast, his strength and voice failed him. In a faultring dying tone, he was just heard to say, " Cut off my head !" and the executioner still lingering, he himself placed his head on the scaffold: in a word, after four strokes with an hatchet, the head was separated from the body, and the body quartered. Such was the end of the renowned Patkul: and may God have mercy on his soul!

LORENS HAGER,
Chaplain of a Regiment.

Such is the account of this dreadful scene, left us by one who was an eye and ear-witness of the whole, and committed it to writing immediately after the thing

hap-

happened. His relation, plain and unadorned as it is, we think still more interesting, more truly moving than the elaborate description given by monsieur de Voltaire, which we therefore omit. We will only add, from that excellent writer, one particular more relating to the unfortunate man, whose terrible exit the reader has just had presented to his view.

Thus perished John Reinold Patkul, ambassador and general of the Russian emperor. Such as saw him only in the light of a subject, in rebellion against his king, thought he had merited the fate he underwent: those who considered him as a Livonian, born in a province that had certain rights and privileges to defend, and called to mind, that he had quitted Livonia, with no other view than to assert those rights, esteemed him a martyr to the liberties of his country. All however agreed, that the title of ambassador from the Czar ought to have rendered his person sacred. The king of

Sweden

Sweden alone, bred up in the principles of despotism, believed, that he had done no more than an act of justice; while all Europe besides, condemned in that act his merciless cruelty.

The quarters of Patkul remained exposed on gibbets till the year seventeen hundred and thirteen; when Augustus, having reascended the throne, gave orders to collect those sad proofs of the extremity he had been reduced to at Altranstad. They were brought before him in a box, to Warsovia, while Buzenval, the French envoy, happened to be present. The king of Poland, directing that minister's eye to the box— there, said he simply, there are the members of Patkul; without adding a single word either in blame or in pity to his memory; and without any one person present daring to open his lips, on a subject so delicate at once and tragical.

THE END.

Printed by Libri Plureos GmbH in Hamburg,
Germany